Anonymous

Seventh Report of the Board of Directors and Officers of the California Institution for the Education of the Deaf and Dumb, and the Blind, to the Governor of the State of California, for the two years ending Sept. 30, 1867.

Anonymous

Seventh Report of the Board of Directors and Officers of the California Institution for the Education of the Deaf and Dumb, and the Blind, to the Governor of the State of California, for the two years ending Sept. 30, 1867.

ISBN/EAN: 9783337184698

Printed in Europe, USA, Canada, Australia, Japan

Cover: Foto ©Andreas Hilbeck / pixelio.de

More available books at **www.hansebooks.com**

SEVENTH REPORT

OF THE

Board of Directors and Officers

OF THE

CALIFORNIA INSTITUTION

FOR THE EDUCATION OF THE

DEAF AND DUMB, AND THE BLIND,

TO THE

Governor of the State of California,

For the two years ending Sept. 30, 1867.

————•◦•————

SAN FRANCISCO:

TURNBULL & SMITH, BOOK AND JOB PRINTERS.
No. 524 Clay Street, next the Market.
1867.

BOARD OF DIRECTORS.

J. P. WHITNEY,......Term expires in 1868.
IRA P. RANKIN,..... " " 1868.
B. H. RANDOLPH,.... " " 1870.
J. A. BENTON,. ...... " " 1870,
WM. SHERMAN,...... " " 1870.

OFFICERS OF THE BOARD.

IRA P. RANKIN, PRESIDENT.   WM. SHERMAN, VICE-PRES'T.
B. H. RANDOLPH, TREASURER.   J. P. WHITNEY, PHYSICIAN.
I. P. RANKIN, AUDITOR.   J. A. BENTON, SECRETARY.

STANDING COMMITTEES.

ON SANITARY REGULATIONS.
J. P. WHITNEY,   I. P. RANKIN.

ON MATTERS OF FINANCE.
B. H. RANDOLPH,   I. P. RANKIN.

ON INSTRUCTION.
WM. SHERMAN,   J. A. BENTON.

VISITING COMMITTEE OF LADIES.

MRS. J. P. WHITNEY,   MRS. B. H. RANDOLPH.
MRS. SAMUEL HORT,   MRS. W. O. ANDREWS.
MRS. DAVID BECK,   MRS. CAPT. E. SMITH.

OFFICERS OF THE INSTITUTION.

INTELLECTUAL DEPARTMENT.

Principal,

WARRING WILKINSON, M.A.

TEACHERS OF THE DEAF AND DUMB,

AMASA PRATT, B. A., HENRY B. CRANDALL, HENRY FRANK.

TEACHER OF DRAWING,

HUBERT BURGESS.

TEACHERS OF THE BLIND,

CHAS. T. WILKINSON, Jr., Miss LOUISE BOWEN.

TEACHER OF MUSIC.

CONSTANTINE MUELLER.

DOMESTIC DEPARTMENT.

Physician,

JAMES P. WHITNEY, M. D.

Matron,

Mrs. EMILY F. AREY.

Assistant Matron,

Mrs. JULIA GRISWOLD.

MECHANICAL DEPARTMENT.

Shoemaker,

CHARLES NUNN.

REPORT OF THE DIRECTORS.

To His Excellency, F. F. Low, Governor of the State of California:

In accordance with an Act of the Legislature of the State of California, approved March 31, 1866, re-organizing the Institution for the education and care of the Deaf and Dumb, and the Blind, and appointing J. P. Whitney, I. P. Rankin, B. H. Randolph, J. A. Benton and William Sherman, Directors of the Institution, we met the 9th day of April, 1866, were qualified according to law, were organized by the choice of I. P. Rankin, for President of the Board; W. Sherman, for Vice-President; B. H. Randolph, for Treasurer; J. P. Whitney, for Physician; and J. A. Benton, for Secretary, and were brought into working order by the adoption of a series of By-Laws, for the government of the Board, and of the Institution.

We have now to report that, ever since this re-organization, we have conducted the affairs of the Institution faithfully, and to the best of our ability, and in accordance with the provisions of the Act aforesaid. We re-elected Prof. W. Wilkinson Principal of the Institution, and confirmed the appointment of the teachers, matron, and other officers and employees nominated by him, under this Act, at the beginning; and, since that time, have done the same whenever vacancies have occurred.

We have held monthly meetings, for hearing reports and for transacting business; have visited the Institution every three months, in person, and given all its departments a thorough examination, and have watched its progress with a tender solicitude and a careful interest.

For the details of the receipts and expenditures of the Institution, and for a full account of its financial affairs, you are respectfully referred to the report of the Treasurer submitted herewith.

For information regarding the interior working of the Institution, the methods of instruction, the distribution of time, the

6

general progress, and the accomplished results, together with all other matters of present importance, you are respectfully referred to the report of the Principal, which will accompany this.

We have been pleased with the ability, assiduity, urbanity and success of the Principal and his assistants, in every department; with the obedience, aptitude, and general good behavior of the pupils ; and with the skill acquired by such as have given a part of their time to mechanical pursuits. To the learning of trades, and to skill in other industries, we hope to be able to direct the attention of the pupils far more largely in the years to come.

The health of the Institution has continued to be remarkably good, especially when it is remembered how crowded the rooms and dormitories have been. The Institution cannot grow, nor even do itself justice, until it has more room, larger grounds, and better facilities. We are glad to believe that there is a good prospect of having all these, in a year or two, through the kindness, liberality, and sense of justice, of the incoming Legislature. And it is our hope that the new edifice for the Institution, already commenced, will be completed and in readiness for the pupils, at the beginning of the next school-year, in August, 1868.

We cannot too warmly commend to yourself, and to all others concerned with the matter of managing and providing for our public institutions of education and of charity, this Institution, whose immediate care has been entrusted to us. It needs fostering. It will repay all benefactions. It is capable of development. It can be made to take a high rank. It is creditable to the State already. It can be made even more honorable to the State than it is already. We even hope for the day when the State shall be proud of it.

Time, toil, means, and all healthful economies will bring it forward. We must earnestly press its claims. We cannot do justice to our views and feelings, without expressing the vehement desire that the State, through all its departments, shall devise and execute liberal things for our wards, the unfortunates, who, without fault of theirs, are, many of them, children of silence—some of them children of night.

Respectfully submitted,

J. A. BENTON,
Secretary.

I. P. RANKIN,
President

REPORT OF THE PRINCIPAL.

To the Board of Directors of the California Institution for the Deaf and Dumb, and the Blind.

GENTLEMEN :—I have the honor hereby to submit the first biennial, corresponding to the eighth annual, report of the California Institution for the Deaf and Dumb, and the Blind, the same being required by section 9 of the Act passed by the last Legislature, and approved March 31, 1866.

At the date of the last report there were under instruction, fifty-five pupils, of whom thirty-six were deaf and dumb, and nineteen were blind. Since then there have been admitted twenty deaf and dumb, including two re-admissions, and twelve blind, including three re-admissions, making a total of eighty-seven pupils under instruction since our last exhibit. Of this number, seventeen have left or from various causes have failed to return on the opening of school. The present number of inmates is therefore seventy.

RECAPITULATION.

No. deaf and dumb at date of last report.............	36	
" " " re-admitted since last report.....	2	
" " " newly admitted " "	18	
Total No. Deaf and Dumb under instruction at date of last report............	56	
No. deaf and dumb who have left since date of last report	8	
" " " now in the Institution...........		48
No. blind at date of last report.....................	19	
" " re-admitted since last report................	3	
" " newly admitted since last report.............	9	
Total No. blind under instruction at date of last report..	31	
No. blind who have left since date of last report........	9	
No. blind now in the Institution.....................		22
Total No. pupils in both departments.................		70

This numerical increase is gratifying as an evidence of public confidence and of enlarged interest in the work we seek to accomplish, but it has taxed to the utmost, our limited accommodations, and proves the wisdom of the last Legislature, in making provision for the purchase of more extensive grounds, and the erection of buildings commensurate with the dignity of the State and the needs of these rapidly increasing unfortunates.

During the annual vacation of 1866, a two-story wooden addition was made to the west building, which served temporarily to relieve our necessities. The first floor was devoted to a kitchen and laundry, and the second floor was appropriated to dormitory uses, while the old kitchen, laundry, and servants' room, were thrown into one, making a dining room. These alterations have added much to the comfort of the pupils, and the convenience of the household, but the crowded condition of the female department still affords cause for constant solicitude, and has compelled us to resort to measures which only necessity can justify.

The first consideration in the management of an educational establishment is, and should be, the health of its inmates. A well nourished and vigorous body is the proper basis for intellectual culture, and no discipline of mind or manners, can compensate for a depreciated tone of the physical system. The tact and address of the teacher may conceal a defective mental training, but no adroitness will serve to hide the sad results of improper sanitary regulations, or a neglected regimen. There are at times, providential interferences, against which human foresight seem to avail nothing. Thus, during the past year three public institutions of learning, the New York Institution for the Deaf and Dumb, the Ohio Institution for the Deaf and Dumb, and Yale College, have been forced to suspend operations by the ravages of the typhoid fever. The reputation of these well managed schools forbids the suspicion of neglect, but their misfortunes serve to increase our gratitude to the All Wise Father, that we are enabled to report a continuance of the remarkable immunity from sickness and death which has been noticed in previous reports of this Institution. For a period of nearly eight years, no death has occurred among our inmates, and during the past two years, there have been only three cases of prolonged and serious illness, two cases of pneumonia, and one of severe fever. In February of the present year, measles of a mild type broke out, and before the disease disappeared, forty pupils were under treatment. By proper medical care and nursing, however, all recovered without experiencing any of those evil effects which too often follow this malady of childhood.

The *personnel* of the Institution, has undergone several changes since our last report. In Feb'y 1866, Miss Meribah Cornell resigned her position as Assistant Matron, and her place was worthily filled by Mrs. Julia Griswold. In April, the appointment of Mr. Charles T. Wilkinson as teacher was approved by the Board, and on the resignation in June of Mrs. Fanny D. Mayne, teacher of the blind,

9

Mr. Wilkinson was placed in charge of that department, where he has discharged his duties with zeal and most gratifying success. In this department we have also had during the year, the assistance of Miss Harriet Lovekin, as teacher of handicraft and reader to the blind. Her place has since been filled by the appointment of Miss Louise Bowen.

In the deaf mute department, such additions have been as serve to render it efficient and progressive. Mr. Hubert Burgess has resumed his connection with the Institution, as teacher of drawing. Mr. Henry Frank, a member of the High Class in the New York Institution, has been appointed a probationary teacher of the Juvenile division, while Mr. Amasa Pratt, a graduate of Williams' College, and for one year, a teacher in the Pennsylvania Institution for the Deaf and Dumb, came out to us in October, and entered at once upon the discharge of his duties with a degree of earnest enthusiasm, which gives the brightest promise of success and eminence in the profession. Mr. Henry B. Crandall still occupies the position he has so long and so worthily filled, while Mrs. Emily F. Arey, the efficient Matron continues to preside over the domestic affairs of the household.

Before dismissing this subject, it is no more than justice to mention the cordial co-operation, I have received from the whole corps of teachers and employees. The management of a public institution, must to a great degree depend for its success upon the zeal and fidelity of the individuals connected therewith in a subordinate capacity, and the superintendent who fails to secure these qualities in his assistants, must inevitably come short of the highest success. It affords me pleasure therefore to say, that throughout all departments, there has been a faithful and earnest labor for the prosperity and welfare of the Institution and its inmates, oftentimes beyond what the strict letter of duty might require, which has been both commendable in itself, and gratifying to me.

The result of this devotion to the work, is seen in the condition of the schools as regards both the intellectual progress, and the *morale* of the pupils. Between teachers and pupils there is free and cordial intercourse without the contempt which proverbially follows familiarity. Prompt obedience is enjoined and rendered, but it is from respect to the law, rather than from fear of the lash. In discipline we prefer to address the conscience, rather than the cuticle. There is more need of restraint from study, than of stimulus thereto. Quarrels and falsehood are almost unknown, save among the younger pupils, whose moral perceptions are not yet awakened, and there is a general development of character, of true manliness and womanliness, in which we find more satisfaction than in any mere monstrosities of learning that might be produced.

We have had numerous evidences during the past two years, of increased confidence and interest in our work, on the part of the community. Many parents and friends of pupils, have visited the Institution, and made themselves personally acquainted with its operations. His Excellency Gov. Low, Hon. John Swett, Superintendent of Public Instruction, and other State officials, have, from time to time, encouraged the pupils, by witnessing their recitations in the class-room, and personally testing the extent of their attainments. A pleasing feature, has been the frequent visits from the principals and teachers of the various City Grammar schools, and we are led to believe that the reputation of the Institution has been advanced thereby.

The close of each academic year, has been attended by an examination and a public exhibition. The examinations were conducted by committees of gentlemen, appointed by the Board, and their condensed reports will be found hereto annexed. The exhibitions were held, one in Platt's Hall, the other in the Academy of Music, before large and appreciative audiences, and netted after paying all expenses, three hundred and sixty-five dollars and thirty-one cents, ($365 31) which sum was generously placed at my disposal, by vote of the Board, to be expended for the benefit of the children. After purchasing a fine set of Appleton's American Cyclopædia, together with other books and amusements for the pupils, to the amount of one hundred and fifteen (115) dollars, a balance of two hundred and fifty-one (251) dollars remains in my hands, which it is purposed to use in making further additions to the Institution library. We hope to repeat these exhibitions from year to year. Their influence on the pupils is beneficial, the people are afforded an opportunity of witnessing the results of an Institution they are taxed to sustain ; and the funds derived therefrom will in time build up a creditable library without expense to the State.

Our thanks are due to B. M. Hartshorne, Esq., of the Cal. Steam Navigation Company ; Gov. Stanford of the Central Pacific, and Sacramento Valley Railroads ; to Charles Minturn, Esq., of the Petaluma Boats, and Messrs. Holliday & Brenham of the Mexican Steamship Company, for courtesies extended to our pupils in going to, and returning from their homes. But for the generosity of these gentlemen in furnishing free passes over their respective routes of travel, many of the pupils by reason of straitened circumstances, would be debarred the privilege of visiting their friends during the vacation, and also lose the benefit of the change of air so desirable after a year's hard study.

Our little shoe shop makes a most favorable exhibit, and gives promise of being remunerative at no distant day. Omitting the salary of the Foreman, which we regard as a legitimate part of the expenditures for instruction, the receipts and expenses have been as follows :

Receipts.

For work done and sold......................$679 37
Finished work and stock on hand............. 80 00
                                            ——— 759 37

11

Expenditures.

Leather and findings...................... 358 06

Balance in favor of shop.............. $401 31

Considering the extremely inconvenient quarters occupied, a mere loft in a small barn, the recent establishment of the shop, and the rawness of the boys, the limited hours available from study and recreation, for mechanical purposes, this result is most encouraging.

No workshop for the blind has as yet been established. In view of our contemplated removal to new premises, it has not been deemed advisable to incur the expense which shop buildings and machinery would involve. Meanwhile, the blind pupils occupy their vacant hours in the manufacture of beadwork, which is sold to the visitors, who may wish specimens of this novel handicraft. The sales since our last report have amounted to $162,67, and the expenditures for material were $41,85, leaving a profit of $120,82.

I feel assured that no extended argument is necessary to impress either the Board of Directors, or the Legislature, with the importance of a well regulated and efficient mechanical department in connection with this Institution. The primary object of education is to develop true manhood ; to subject to the higher law of our being, all the powers and faculties of the soul, and to inculcate such a discipline as shall fit and prepare one for any and all duties. We would so educate as to make every man an Argus and Briareus combined, hundred-eyed, and hundred-handed, quick to perceive, and facile to execute what the exigencies of life may require. As a general rule, special instruction in handicraft should follow the intelligence developed in the school room, but the peculiar deprivations of the deaf and dumb, and the blind, render them ineligible for the terms of ordinary apprenticeship. Few master mechanics are willing to incur the irksome labor of teaching those who are bereft of sight or hearing. Moreover, our pupils do not graduate before the age of eighteen or twenty, when the hand lacking somewhat the suppleness of youth, finds difficulty in adapting itself to the use of tools or the exercise of a mechanical pursuit.

For these reasons, the instruction in some useful industry, whereby the young graduate may relieve his friends from the burden of his support, and add his share to the productive wealth of the State, has been the wise, as well as humane, policy of all institutions of this character; and I most earnestly recommend that liberal provision for this department be made in connection with the new buildings now erecting.

Since the Sixth Annual Report was published, many radical changes have taken place in the legal, as well as financial, status of the Institution. Up to that date, the Institution seemed to be regarded as a natural, rather than as a legitimate, child of the

State, whose claim for support was only partially allowed. The appropriations were meagre, and were doled as a charity, rather than as the satisfaction of a just demand upon the State revenues. The unfortunate children had the stigma of an exceptional treatment, while the efficiency of the Institution was impaired by its limited resources.

The liberal measures adopted by the last Legislature changed all this, and raised the Institution to the dignity and importance which its work and prospective increase justify. A law abolishing the incongruities of past legislation, and defining the duties and responsibilities of Directors and Principal, was enacted, by which the Institution is placed on an equality with other State establishments. The Directors receive a compensation, which, however meagre it may be, is an acknowledgement that they render a service to the commonwealth ; the appropriation, $25,000 per annum, has proved sufficient for the conduct of the Institution. The inmates are, under the present law, considered as the children of the State, and, as such, entitled to the education which California wisely provides for all. Their stay, which was formerly limited to five years, is now practically unlimited; and the unhappy distinctions between rich and poor are abolished by throwing open our doors to all deaf and dumb, and blind children of suitable age, residents of California.

These, with the Bill and appropriation relating to the erection of new buildings, are the main features of the legislation in our behalf at the last session. That legislation I believe to have been wise, liberal, just; and, carried out in the same spirit by the management, cannot fail of accomplishing beneficent results for those whom this Institution was established to educate.

The Board of Commissioners, appointed to locate and erect new buildings for the use of the deaf and dumb, and the blind, will doubtless make a report detailing the proceedings of the Commission. Our own record, however, would be incomplete without some reference to an event so important in the history of this Institution as its removal and permanent location.

The Commissioners met for organization on the tenth day of April 1866, and after qualifying according to law, entered at once upon the discharge of their duties. In answer to advertisements inserted in various and widely-circulated papers, numerous sites were offered, all of which the Board visited. After mature deliberation, the Commissioners unanimously decided upon a tract of 130 acres, known as the "Kearney Farm," situated four miles north of Oakland, adjoining the premises belonging to the College of California. The wisdom of this selection has been approved by every unbiased person who has seen it, and also by the recent location of the State Agricultural College in its immediate vicinity. It combines a fruitful soil; a bountiful supply of pure water, from a source sufficiently high to carry the water by natural flow into the third story of the projected building; an elevation which affords opportunity for easy and rapid drainage; a climate possessing all the freshness and salubrity of the coast country, without the sharp summer winds of San Francisco or the debilitating heats of the interior; and an outlook over a varied and extensive landscape and water-view of surpassing loveliness. It lies directly in front of the Golden Gate, through which we look upon the heaving, restless ocean, with all its solemn mysteries and suggestions, and see the long lines of smoke which herald the coming steamers and the white-winged fleets of commerce, long before they are visible to the Queen City of the Pacific. It seems appropriate thus to grace the very threshold of the State with an imposing structure devoted to benevolent uses. It is like the "*salve*" on the old Roman door-step—indicative of the generous disposition of our people; and cannot fail to impress all new-comers to our shores with the worth of a civilization whose first care is the relief of the unfortunate.

Among a variety of plans offered to the Commissioners in response to advertisements, those of Messrs. Wright and Sanders were accepted. A description of the designs, copied from a San Francisco journal, will be found in an appendix to this report. I would merely state in this connection, that the architects have succeeded beyond expectation in planning a symmetrical building, which enables us to isolate the blind from the deaf and dumb, and yet brings all departments under the immediate supervision and control of one Principal.

It was determined to erect the building of an excellent quality of blue stone, found in the neighborhood; and the contract for masonry was let to J. S. Emory, while the contracts for carpentry, plastering, painting, etc., were let to J. J. Macready. Ground was broken on the 29th of July, and on the 26th of September the corner-stone was laid in the presence of a goodly number of ladies and gentlemen, and about fifty pupils from the Institution. The following was the order of exercises on that occasion :

1. Introductory Address by Ira P. Rankin. President of the Board of Commissioners.
2. Prayer by Rev. A. L. Stone, D.D.
3. Address by Warring Wilkinson. Principal of the Institution.
4. Ode written for the occasion by Mr. Frank Bret Harte, and read by Hon. John Swett.
5. Reading of the list of articles deposited in the jar, by Rev. J. A. Benton.
6. Depositing the jar in the corner-stone.
7. Laying the corner-stone, and Address by His Excellency Gov. F. F. Low.
8. Extempore Addresses by Rev. Dr. Stone, Rev. Mr. Beckwith, Senator Robinson, of Alameda, Hon. Edward Tompkins, and Rev. Mr. Willey.
9. Collation, prepared by Mrs. Emory and other ladies.

Since the laying of the corner-stone, the work has been prosecuted with commendable diligence; and at this present writing, the walls, with the exception of the front, are ready for the second floor joists. The character of the workmanship, and the quality of the materials, thus far, indicate that the contractors are more ambitious for their reputation as builders than for pecuniary profit,and we have the authority of unprejudiced and competent judges for the statement, that at the estimated cost of one hundred and fifty thousand dollars, which is the total for grounds, buildings, heating and gas apparatus, it will be the cheapest structure in California.

It may not be generally known that this Institution is designed to supply for many years the educational facilities for all the deaf and dumb and the blind of the Pacific coast. His Excellency Gov. Wood, of Oregon, has visited our schools, and being satisfied that we can educate the unfortunates of Oregon cheaper and better than they can do it at home, has kindly promised to urge upon the next Legislature of that State the propriety of making suitable provision for the support of their indigent deaf and dumb, and blind, in this Institution. I shall also, with the consent of the Board, take measures to bring the subject before the Legislature of Nevada, and have no doubt that the citizens of that State will avail themselves of the privileges and benefits which we are enabled to offer at most reasonable rates. It is in expectation of meeting the needs of sister States that our buildings have been planned on a liberal and generous scale. By gathering the deaf and dumb, and the blind of all the coast into one institution, we not only decrease the expense *pro rata* for our own children, but are enabled to increase the efficiency of the schools by a more perfect classification than is possible with small numbers ; by the greater variety of trades offered for the choice and adaptation of the pupils, and by the co-operation of a larger corps of intelligent instructors.

It is well known to all members of the profession that deaf mute instruction in America has been reduced to a science almost as exact as mathematics. It is no longer an experiment or an untested theory. It is the legitimate result of a hundred years well directed search for truth, by unselfish men possessing at least an ordinary degree of intelligence, and actuated by an unusual singleness of purpose. It is the thoughtfully settled conviction of every prominent member of the profession in the United States, and there is probably no class of men so nearly unanimous in sentiment as teachers of the deaf and dumb.

This method is based upon the French system of signs, the primal idea of which is that words are arbitrary symbols, and no more essential to the expression of thought than the nine digits are essential to the statement of mathematical ideas. It is unfortunate that the terms speech and language, are used synonymously. Speech is really the articulate utterance of intelligible sounds, while language is a mere general term, and whatever its etymological derivation may be, has come to mean any symbolism by which the inner thought is made outward, and may be addressed to the eye, as in the case of writing or signs. Language, that is the use of symbols to express thought, is necessary to mental development, but speech is not absolutely essential thereto, and when it is artificial as in the case of parrots and magpies it is no evidence of intelligence. Accepting this distinction, we perceive the fundamental error of the German teacher Samuel Heinicke, who established a school for the deaf and dumb in Saxony contemporaneously with the Abbe de l'Epee in Paris. Heineckeheld that without speech, there could be no mental development, and therefore devoted all his art and energies to imparting to his pupils an artificial articulation. His system has found acceptance in most of the German schools, and prevails there at the present day.

During the last two years a warm discussion has been carried on in various prominent journals at the East, elicited by the proposed introduction into American schools for the deaf and dumb of this method. The measure has found most earnest advocates. Because these advocates are, without exception we believe, men practically unacquainted with the present modes in vogue among deaf mute instructors is no conclusive argument that they are wrong. Neither is an isolated case or two of successful articulation conclusive evidence that they are right. The discussion has now culminated in what we have long desired to see, the establishment of a school, at Northampton, Mass., where the system is to be tried under the auspices of those who ardently believe in the practability of teaching articulation. We need no further argument, but rather a comparison of results, not between Germany and America where the results are obtained in diverse languages, and translated into the exaggerated hyperboles of inexperienced visitors, but between Northampton and Hartford or New York, where pupils educated in the use of a common language can be brought face to face, in the presence of professional experts. Let the test be for mental development, and not for parrot utterances, and if that test prove the superiority of the German system over the American, we can assure the able Chairman of the Massachusetts Board of State Charities, that no professional pride will prevent the speedy introduction of that system into the California school for the deaf and dumb.

In closing this report, I desire to express my grateful appreciation of the confidence and cordial co-operation, I have received from the Board since our connection. The assurances which you gave me on my arrival, have been more than fulfilled. If any thing has been done during the past two years to advance the prosperity of the Institution, it is largely due to your liberal policy. If any thing has not been done for its efficiency, that might well have been done, the fault and responsibility are mine.

Respectfully submitted,

WARRING WILKINSON,

Principal.

Institution for the Deaf and Dumb, and the Blind, }
    San Francisco, Sept. 30, 1867. }

TREASURER'S ACCOUNT.

For Groceries and Provisions.

Allspice.....................................$	1	40
Barley..	3	01
Bath-brick...................................		75
Beans, 385 lbs..............................	15	21
Beeswax.....................................		25
Berries.......................................	14	35
Blueing.......................................	9	30
Bread...	67	98
Buckwheat...................................	7	75
Butter, 2,723½ lbs.........................	975	47
Dried Fruit..................................	4	55
Cake..	2	85
Carraway Seed..............................		25
Cassia..	4	38
Catsup..	2	45
Cheese, 495½ lbs...........................	73	55
Citron..		50
Codfish.......................................	18	23
Coffee, 598 lbs..............................	144	56
Corn starch..................................	5	52
Crackers.....................................	44	39
Cracked wheat..............................		50
Cranberries..................................	9	00
Cream Tartar...............................	6	45
Eggs, 182½ doz..............................	69	90
Fish...	74	60
Flour, 148½ lbs..............................	876	39
Fruit..	171	28
Ginger..	5	75
Ham, 142 lbs................................	25	34
Honey..	1	00
Hops..	21	35
Ice..		10
Jelly..	2	57
Carried forward	2660	93

17

Brought forward....	2660	93
Lard, 403 lbs.....................	72	96
Lemons and extracts............	8	50
Mackerel, 2 kits....................	6	00
Meal.................................	7	00
Meats, 19,403 lbs...................	1,809	86
Milk................................	12	40
Mustard............................	11	85
Nutmegs............................	3	20
Oranges............................	1	00
Oysters............................	26	15
Peas...............................	6	95
Pepper.............................	13	50
Pickles............................	19	50
Pork...............................	83	25
Potash.............................		25
Poultry............................	35	65
Raisins............................	9	50
Rice, 250 lbs......................	21	50
Resin..............................		85
Salad oil..........................	1	55
Saleratus..........................	2	15
Salt...............................	11	95
Sausages...........................	17	40
Shrimp.............................		20
Smoked beef........................	40	50
Soap, brown, 1,421½ lbs............	117	24
Soap, castile, 104 lbs.............	18	51
Starch.............................	21	75
Sugar, brown, 3,154 lbs............	356	28
Sugar, crushed, 698 lbs............	101	61
Syrup, 178½ gals...................	131	03
Tea, 184 lbs.......................	144	05
Tongues............................	3	50
Vegetables.........................	885	66
Vinegar............................	60	02
Washing Powder.....................	41	30
Wheat..............................		50
Worcester sauce....................		50
Yeast and yeast powders............	15	05
		6,781 55

Salaries and Wages.

Principal and Teachers............10,986	63	
Directors and Treasurer	1,500	00
Physician, Matron and Assistant........	2,588	75
Servants and service..................	2,642	20
Foreman of shoe-shop..................	1,020	00
		18,737 58

Carried forward.... .... 25,519 13

18

Clothing.

Brought forward................... 25,519 13

Alpaca, 44 yds....................	21	50
Batting, 35 lbs....................	12	00
Beeswax.........................		10
Belts, 2.........................	1	00
Blacking and Brushes..............	13	45
Boots and Shoes, 6 prs............	12	88
Braid,...........................	5	46
Buckles..........................	1	75
Buttons,.........................	16	46
Calico, 359¼ yds.................	58	70
Cambric, 35 yds..................	6	55
Canvas, 2yds.....................	1	00
Caps, 25.........................	22	13
Cassimere, 107 yds...............	119	82
Check Muslin, 5 yds..............	3	00
Coats, 7.........................	30	50
Coat Binding.....................	1	75
Combs...........................	15	27
Cotton Cloth, 194¾ yds...........	72	44
Crotchet Needles,................		75
Cutting,.........................	2	50
Delaine, 6 yds...................	2	25
Denham, 15½ yds.................	3	90
Drilling, 34 yds..................	9	14
Drawers, 8 prs...................	7	75
Elastic,.........................	6	30
Empress Cloth, 3 yds.............	4	00
Eyelets,.........................		50
Flannel, 8 yds...................	4	75
Gaiters, 16 prs..................	28	25
Girls Hats, 8....................	15	75
Gloves, 15 prs...................	4	15
Hair Oil,........................	1	25
Hair Pins,.......................		35
Handkerchiefs, 13½ doz...........	16	77
Hats, 25.........................	30	25
Hooks and Eyes...................	1	15
Hoopskirts, 25	23	30
Hose, 133 prs....................	45	50
Illusion,........................		25
Kentucky Jean, 34½ yds...........	13	59
Knitting Cotton,.................		40
Linen, 7 yds.....................	5	00
Machine Needles,.................	3	10
Making Dress,....................	3	50

Carried forward.......... 650 16   25,519 13

Brought forward..........	650 16	25,519 13
Marking Ink,.........................	2 80	
Merino, 7½ yds......................	7 80	
Muslin 256 yds......................	68 60	
Nets, 12	5 75	
Needles.............................	4 63	
Neckties,...........................	5 25	
Pantaloons, 3 prs....................	10 00	
Pins................................	2 20	
Poplin, 18½ yds	18 50	
Pressing Hats.......................	2 80	
Repairing,..........................	2 00	
Ribbon..............................	4 85	
Ruffling............................	60	
Scissors	3 87	
Sewing Silk.........................	90	
Shawls, 2...........................	3 25	
Shirts, 85,.........................	111 50	
Shoestrings	2 70	
Silk,...............................	2 63	
Socks, 55 prs.......................	15 12	
Stockings, 16 prs...................	5 42	
Suspenders, 30 prs..................	8 75	
Suits, 11...........................	167 00	
Tape,...............................	25	
Tarleton, 93¼ yds...................	31 61	
Thimbles,...........................	65	
Thread..............................	35 60	
Trimming,...........................	30	
Twist...............................	30	
Undershirts, 4......................	5 50	
Vails...............................	50	
Velvet Ribbon.......................	4 80	
Wadding.............................	85	
Woolen Plaid, 30 yds................	19 79	
Worsted.............................	35	
Wages of Seamstress.................	104 50	
Yarn................................	6 60	
		1318 68

Furniture.

Baskets.............................	3 90	
Beds, 9.............................	40 00	
Bedsteads, 21.......................	101 00	
Bedwrenches.........................	85	
Bells...............................	1 75	
Blackboards and fixtures	7 10	
Carried forward..........	154 60	26,837 81

Brought forward	154 60	26,837 81
Blankets, 27 prs	124 00	
Boilers, 3	16 00	
Bookcases, 3	68 00	
Box Benches, 2	9 50	
Bread table and board	7 00	
Bread Knives	2 75	
Bread Trays	2 00	
Brooms, 5½ doz	30 25	
Brushes	2 00	
Carpet, 73 yds	135 53	
Carving Set	5 00	
Castors	70	
Chairs, 44	52 00	
Chopping Knife	25	
Clothes Baskets	11 50	
Clothes Lines and pins	8 85	
Clothes Wringer	8 50	
Coal hods and shovels	4 75	
Coal Screens	1 25	
Coffee Mills	1 75	
Corkscrew	50	
Cots, 7	22 50	
Cotton Batting	4 50	
Crash, 101½ yds	16 55	
Crockery	70 28	
Curtains and fixtures	77 98	
Desk, (office)	50 00	
Desks, teachers'	30 00	
Desks, school. 4	28 00	
Dusters	4 95	
Dust Pans	2 95	
Glue	25	
Hatchet	2 50	
Jars	3 60	
Knives and Forks	32 00	
Locks	8 00	
Lining, 30 yds	4 50	
Looking Glasses	10 00	
Match safes	50	
Matting, 75 yds	44 84	
Mattresses, 13	54 50	
Mops	1 50	
Napkins, 5 doz	13 00	
Oil Cloth, 52 yds	51 47	
Pails	3 20	
Pillows	29 50	
Carried forward	1,213 75	26,837 81

Brought forward	1,213 75	26,837 81
Pulleys	75	
Quilts, 32	81 00	
Range, furniture, etc	286 70	
Rep, clocks	3 00	
Rep. furniture	58 87	
Rubber cloth	2 00	
Scales	18 00	
Screws	25	
Screw driver	50	
Screw wrench	2 00	
Scrubbing brushes	2 15	
Settees, 6	36 00	
Sheeting, 239 yds	88 99	
Shovel	25	
Spoons	9 25	
Stair rods	5 62	
Stools, 60	30 00	
Stove blacking	1 95	
Stoves and furniture	90 28	
Straw beds	11 00	
Tables	83 00	
Table Covers	5 00	
Table Linen, 10 yds	13 35	
Tacks	1 55	
Ticking, 74 yds	17 44	
Tinners' bill	12 85	
Tinware and rep. do	34 05	
Towels	7 50	
Washstands, 2	10 00	
Wire screen	1 40	
Wooden ware	5 35	
		2133 80

Books and Stationery, etc.

Arithmetical Frame	5 00	
Account Books	6 60	
Bibles and books for the blind	82 15	
Blank Books	8 75	
Blotters	1 75	
Ciphering Boards and type for blind, 10	48 24	
Copy Books	4 50	
Crayons, 35 boxes	20 40	
Dictionaries, Webster's, 2	20 13	
Drawing Materials	13 60	
Envelopes	9 42	
Ink	1 73	
Carried forward	222 27	28,971 61

Brought forward	222 27	28,971 61
Liquid slating........................	3 00	
Maps..................................	15 50	
Mucilage..............................	75	
Numerical Frame......................	1 69	
Pasteboard............................	50	
Pens..................................	1 00	
Penholders............................	50	
Penrack...............................	1 00	
School Books..........................	47 40	
Slates and Pencils....................	10 37	
Stationery............................	28 62	
		332 60

Building and Repairs.

Bell hanging..........................	11 00	
Brass hooks...........................	25	
Building new kitchen and laundry......	1775 00	
Carpenters work......................	41 75	
Cleaning Vaults.......................	100 00	
Clothes hooks.........................	3 75	
Doors and hanging do.................	28 50	
Door springs.........................	3 00	
Gates................................	10 00	
Glass and setting.....................	17 73	
Hinges...............................	55	
Hitching Posts........................	3 00	
Locks................................	75	
Lumber...............................	72 36	
Making Sewers........................	165 60	
Nails and screws......................	8 70	
Painting..............................	142 05	
Plastering............................	35 00	
Plumbers bill.........................	379 30	
Repairs..............................	74 50	
Shovel................................	1 50	
Tinners Bill..........................	23 38	
Whitening............................	122 50	
Window fastenings....................	1 00	
Wood shed............................	30 00	
		3051 17

Fuel and Lights.

Burners, 2............................	75	
Candles, 207 lbs......................	50 00	
Candlesticks, 3.......................	2 25	
Carried forward	53 00	32,355 38

Brought forward..........	53 00	32,355 38
Charcoal.....	75	
Chimnies..	17 12	
Coal, 43 tons.	686 50	
Coal oil, 230 galls	170 00	
Coke.	5 00	
Lamps..	31 75	
Lamp shade.	1 00	
Matches.	10 47	
Wicks..	2 25	
Wood, 23 cords.	249 25	
		1227 09

Stable.

Barley, 94 lbs.	1 08	
Bran, 9739 lbs.	79 68	
Brooms, 2.	2 75	
Hay, 22,801 lbs.	172 40	
Oats 2,241 lbs.	36 61	
Straw,	2 00	
		294 52

Miscellaneous.

Axe Helves.	2 60	
Bergamot,	25	
Bill Heads.	3 00	
Blacksmithing,	12 25	
Building Bulkhead.	200 00	
Cartage	35 00	
Car Tickets and Traveling expenses	80 45	
Cash advanced to pupils.	233 12	
Chloride of Lime	3 30	
Cleaning Chimneys.	3 00	
Cow.	92 50	
Cutting Hair.	6 50	
Cutting Grass.	1 00	
Directory.	5 00	
Expenses, delegation of pupils to Sacramento, by invitation of Legislature,....	175 00	
Expenses of pupils going home.	35 50	
Express charges.	19 75	
Error,	4 00	
Filing Saw,	25	
Filling Lot,.	175 00	
Flaxseed,	75	
Glue.	1 15	
Interest,	303 16	
Leather and Findings,	358 06	
Carried forward..........	1,750 59	33,876 99

Brought forward............	1,750 59	33,876 99
Lime,...........................	2 50	
Machine Needles,....................	1 00	
Material for Beadwork,...............	41 85	
Medicines,.........................	228 15	
Music and Music strings....	41 64	
Notary's Fees	8 00	
Post Box, Stamps, etc................	41 07	
Printing.........................	108 12	
Raising fence	200 00	
Rat and Fly Poison...................	1 90	
Receipts	2 00	
Rent of Office.....................	175 00	.
Rep. Instruments	11 15	
Rep. Organ	80 00	
Rep. and Tuning Pianos...............	78 00	
Rep. Sewing Machine.............	1 00	
Scythe Stones	30	
Seeds............................	1 95	
Services of Architect.................	85 00	
Sewing Machine.....................	65 00	
Shovels,..........................	3 00	
Sickle...........................	1 25	
Sponge...	50	
Street Assessments..................	1375 00	
Syringe............................	2 25	
Telegraphing	8 50	
Triangle Rule..................... .	2 50	
T Square	1 25	
Twine,...........................	50	
Use of Bull.........................	1 00	
Water............................	525 00	
Wheelbarrow	4 50	
		4,849 47
		38,726 46
Balance from last Report...............		24 98
		38,751 44

RECEIPTS.

From State Treasurer for Jan. 1866	⎫	
" " " Feb. "	⎬	3,312 50
" " " March "	⎭	
" " " April "		2,116 65
" " " May " ...		2,116 65
" " " June "		1,142 17
Carried forward..........		8,687 97

		Brought forward			....	8,687	97	
From State Treasurer for July				"	....	1,800	00	
"	"	"	August	"	....	1,800	00	
"	"	"	Sept.	"	....	1,800	00	
"	"	"	Oct.	"	...	1,783	34	
"	"	"	Nov.	"	....	1,783	33	
"	"	"	Dec.	"	....	1,783	33	
"	"	"	Jan.	1867....		1,900	00	
"	"	"	Feb.	"	.?..	1,900	00	
"	"	"	March	"	....	1,900	00	
"	"	"	April	"	....	2,850	00	
"	"	"	May	"	····	2,850	00	
"	"	"	June	"	....	2,850	00	
"	"	"	July	"	....	1,816	67	
						35,504	64	
From pay pupils from Oregon......................						1,184	45	
" pupils for clothing and cash furnished....					..	1,079	64	
" sales of beadwork.............................						162	67	
" custom work in shoe shop..................						235	14	
" sale of cow and calf........................						51	10	
" sale of bags, oil cases, etc..................						28	90	
" miscellaneous sources.....................						9	90	
						38,256	44	
Balance due Treasurer Oct. 1st, 1867......						495	00	
						$38,751	44	

LIST OF PUPILS

In the Institution, since January 1st, 1866.

DEAF AND DUMB.

MALES.

Names.	Town	County.
Ballard, Byron	San Jose	Santa Clara
Bassett. James A.	Sonoma	Sonoma
Benjamin. Brazilliar	San Francisco	San Francisco
Bently. John W.	Albany	Linn. Oregon
Blish, Preston	San Francisco	San Francisco
Butler, Millard F.	Marysville	Yuba
Colby, Edwin	Stony Point	Sonoma
Devoe, Henry	San Francisco	San Francisco
DeRutte, Theophilus	San Francisco	San Francisco
Dickson, Henry A.	Putab	Solano
Gayou, Marcelin	Stockton	San Joaquin
Gibert, Hippolite	Mariposa	Mariposa
Giddings. Henry R.	Woodland	Yolo
Harlan. James C.	Yuba	Sutter
Hill, Mahlon S.		Merced
Hill. Eldridge B.		Merced
Holding. John A.	Stockton	San Joaquin
Hull. Frank	Hicksville	Sacramento
Ide, L. H. C.	San Francisco	San Francisco
Krautz, Louis.	San Francisco	San Francisco
Larue, John	Peoria	Linn. Oregon
Lindsay, John	Windsor	Sonoma
Markham. Columbia	Suisun	Solano
McKail, James Jr.	Sacramento	Sacramento
Murphy, Preston	Napa	Napa
Musgrave, James R.	Point Arenas	Mendocino
Nichols, Henry	Pacheco	Contra Costa
O'Brien, James P.	San Francisco	San Francisco
O'Farrel. Garret	San Francisco	San Francisco
Phillips, William M.	Yreka	Siskiyou
Robison, John W.	San Francisco	San Francisco
Sandercock, Thomas Y.	Napa	Napa
Santa Cruz, Jose	San Francisco	San Francisco
Shattuck, Frank B.	San Francisco	San Francisco
Slater. George	Placerville	El Dorado
Smith, Charles	Georgetown	El Dorado
Tilden, Douglas	Chico	Butte
Willsie, Joseph F.		Marin
Wright, Albert H.	San Francisco	San Francisco

FEMALES.

Aronsohn, Caroline............ ......San Francisco.......San Francisco........
Badger, Harriet F.............. ....Sacramento.........Sacramento........
Douglas, Caroline.................Visalia..............Tulare............
Hard, Amy E.....................Antioch...........Contra Costa.......
King, Eliza A....................Oakland..........Alameda..........
May, America....................Petaluma.........Sonoma...........
May, Anna.......................Petaluma.........Sonoma...........
McKail, Mary....................Sacramento........Sacramento........
McTigue, Augusta................San Francisco.......San Francisco......
Nolan, Mary.....................San Francisco.......San Francisco......
Rogers, Mary Adella............Woodland..........Yolo.............
Shirley, Evadne..................Stockton..........San Joaquin.......
Theobald, Catherine.............Sheldon...........Sacramento........
Uhl, Anna Margaret..............San Francisco.......San Francisco......
Wilts, Mary Louisa..............Lafayette.........Contra Costa........
Wertheimer, Susan...............San Francisco...... San Francisco.......
Wright, Mary....................San Francisco.......San Francisco.......

BLIND.

MALES.

Bennet, Eugene.................. Fremont.......... Yolo.............
Briggs, Eugene A.................Visalia............Tulare............
Caliseb, Levi F..................Sacramento........Sacramento........
Campbell, Henry.................San Francisco.......San Francisco......
Hanley, James Edward...........Oakland..........Alameda..........
Joice, James....................San Luis Obispo....
Jones, Charles J................Grass Valley.......Nevada ....
Knobloch, Charles...............San Francisco.......San Francisco......
Lawrence, F. A..................San Francisco.......San Francisco......
Lerch, Charles..................San Francisco.......San Francisco......
Lerch, Emille...................San Francisco.......San Francisco......
Miller, Peter...................Dry Creek.........Yuba.............
Smith, William H................Santa Cruz........Santa Cruz.........
Thresher, Prescott B............Hamilton ....Butte ....

FEMALES.

Baily, Daisy A..................San Francisco.......San Francisco.......
Brissell, Anna M.................Sacramento.........Sacramento ....
Borgwardt, Mary A...............Kelsey............El Dorado..........
Dunning, Alice..................Watsonville........Santa Cruz.........
Fennel, Anna....................San Francisco.......San Francisco.......
Heryford, Missouri A.............Lincoln...........Placer............
Jenkins, Isabella................San Francisco.......San Francisco.......
Keener, Sarah M.................Visalia.......Tulare............
Kelly, Eloise...................Marysville.........Yuba.............
Klink, Maggie J.................Windsor ....Sonoma...........
Lovell, Laura...................San Jose..........Santa Clara.........
Lowenberg, Virginia.............San Francisco ......San Francisco.......
Mackenthaler, Louisa............San Francisco ......San Francisco.......
Miles, Mary E...................Rio Vista.........Solano...........
Moran, Mary E..................San Francisco.......San Francisco.......
Morgan, Zuratha S...............Horsetown.........Shasta ....
Taft, Sophia A..................San Francisco.......San Francisco.......

28

SUMMARY.

Deaf and Dumb. — Males...................................... 39
"   "   Females 17
                                                                ——— 56
Blind — Males... 14
"   Females 17
                                                                ——— 31

Total...............................   87

REPORT OF THE COMMITTEE OF EXAMINATION

FOR 1866.

To the Directors of the California Institution for the Deaf and Dumb, and the Blind.

The undersigned, having acted as Examiners of the Institution under your charge, beg leave to submit the following report :

The deaf and dumb under instruction in the Institution are thirty-six in number. Of these, twenty-seven are males, and nine females. They are of various ages, from six years up to twenty.

The Committee of Examination found these pupils assembled in the two school-rooms appropriated to their use. These rooms are of good size, well lighted and ventilated, and suitably furnished with desks, seats, and black-boards.

The more advanced scholars occupy one room, and are under the immediate care and tuition of the Principal himself. The other, which may be called the Primary Department, occupying the second room, is taught by Mr. H. B. Crandall, himself a deaf mute, and a graduate of the New York Institution for the Instruction of the Deaf and Dumb.

The Committee were first introduced into this second room. Here were twenty-two pupils—thirteen males and nine females. Some of them had been under instruction for only a few months, and some of them for more than a year. They were of all the varieties of age that have been before mentioned, evidently of great variety of capacity, and of course of every grade of profi-ciency. It is obvious that this variety must complicate the task of the teacher. Very few general instructions, adapted to all in the teacher's presence, can be imparted. Classification is impossible. If at all exact, it would reduce each grade to a numerical representation of one. The teacher was in fact obliged to individualize his method and treatment, giving his attention in turn to each pupil under his care, and conducting with each a separate process suited to the case. There is great want of economy in the outlay of the time and strength thus expended, but it seems unavoidable in the present state of the Institution.

The Committee were gratified with the evidences of docility and progress in the pupils of this department. Those least advanced could translate from the teacher's signs, and spell out the manual alphabet, or write on the black-board such simple phrases and sentences as the following :

> " A blue box."
> " A red book."
> " I see a black hat."

Those more developed wrote longer sentences, involving more difficult idioms, and higher grammatical principles. The ideas were communicated

by the teacher in signs, with no dictation of language, and expressed by the
pupils in language of their own choice and composition. In some instances
these ideas were simple historical facts, and were rendered by the pupils with
a facility and correctness which showed that they had become familiar with
them.

The handwriting of most of the pupils in this room was remarkably neat and
legible. Their manner was that of happy and contented children, pleased to
learn, and eager to make progress.

The pupils in the other room, under Professor Wilkinson's tuition, were
fourteen in number, all males. They had been under instruction from three
to five years, though some of them had not reached the age of twelve. They
were examined, in the first place, in geography, and gave, with perfect accuracy,
many of the more elaborate and extended geographical definitions ; computed
the latitude and longitude of localities ; wrote out, rapidly, long catalogues of
the principal countries, mountains, rivers, and cities of the world, and named
from the charts exhibited before them the salient features of each division of
land and water on the globe.

They were next taken into the domain of history, and showed, as far as they
had progressed in that study, a familiarity with many dates and events that
went rather beyond the memory of the examiners. A single phrase given them
to test their ability to compose and generalize, like " The Mayflower," " Bunker
Hill," " Yorktown," etc., brought out from them connected and graceful narra-
tives of the events grouped around those key-words. They were often interro-
gated by the Committee to see if they understood the language which they
employed, or were only using it as parrots or copyists. These experiments
invariably issued to the pupil's credit, and bore witne-s to the thoroughness
and conscientiousness with which their advance had been conducted. In these
compositions there was a remarkable freedom from the inverted, involved and
confused idioms which are so often observed in the written language of the
deaf and dumb. Nothing but great painstaking on the part of the instructor
could have secured for those who have never listened to the idioms of spoken
language, and whose natural order of communication by signs is the poetic or
inverted order, the easy mastery of so pure and correct a style.

Of the examination in grammar, the Committee only feel competent to express
their admiration. The system devised by Dr. Barnard, of New York, and introduced here by Professor Wilkinson, is so complicated in its appearance, yet
so philosophical in its symbolism and so practical in its results, as to require
more space for its elucidation than the present report allows. By this system
the study of language becomes an exact science, and analysis is carried to a
mathematical demonstration. In testing its practical application, long sentences were analyzed with an ease and minute correctness that would have been
creditable in a college graduate. Symbolic formulas were given, involving
relative, participial and adverbial clauses, infinitives used as subject and object
of finite verbs, etc., all of which were written with surprising accuracy.

The Committee are satisfied, from their own observation, as well as from
general considerations, of the wisdom of sending deaf and dumb children to
the Institution at a much earlier age than that prescribed in the older institutions of the country. Many of the brightest and most forward scholars of this

Institution were under the age of twelve, the point at which some of the oldest schools of the kind at the East open their doors for the admission of new pupils. We think our Legislature has acted wisely in placing no restriction upon this matter, but leaving it to be controlled by the judgment of those in charge of the Institution and the wishes of parents and guardians. The flexibility and docility of these earlier years are priceless advantages in securing a timely and liberal intellectual growth and furnishing.

Before closing their report of this department, the Committee desire to express their gratification at the fine specimens of shoemaking exhibited as the work of the pupils. The shoes were all strongly and neatly made, and gave evidence that these deaf mutes can apply the culture acquired in the class-room to a productive industry.

THE DEPARTMENT OF THE BLIND.

In the department of the blind are twenty-three pupils—eleven males and twelve females—from eight to twenty years of age. They are under the immediate superintendence of Mrs. Fanny Mayne. The tidy and well-cared for appearance of these children is worthy of notice and commendation. Their misfortune is not as great as that of the deaf, yet they are not so well qualified to care for their personal habits of cleanliness and dress. Sight is not the most precious sense, but the want of it has peculiar embarrassments, among the most manifest and outward of which is a depreciated tone of personal habits. To inspire the inward sense of neatness and good taste, is the invention of a higher faculty to make good the lost power. In the teaching of this department the same difficulty holds as in the department of the deaf—disparity of age and pupilage—which time and increased numbers alone can overcome.

The classes brought forward for examination conversed with intelligence and fluency. In spelling and defining they were quick and appreciative, and could define their definitions. They talked about grammar and the construction of sentences with facility and intelligent zest. They were ready in mental arithmetic : gave the cost of a morning's marketing with great quickness, smiling to think anybody supposed *that* was a trial of their powers. They were then asked to compute the interest of $500 for one year three months and fifteen days, which they did, showing at once their patient intelligence and alacrity. They were equally intelligent in geography, and had a correct conception of place and distance on the terrestrial sphere. They enjoyed the examination and seemed sorry to have it end.

The appearance of this department is more than satisfactory, not only in its present condition, but in its prospects.

In closing their report, the Committee cannot omit to express their great satisfaction with the whole appearance of the Institution, and the spirit which pervades it. If vocation, enthusiasm and practical sagacity are any pledge of success, or any promise of distinguished usefulness and beneficence, then the Directors may have new cause of confidence and hope. The Committee feel that the Directors cannot commend the Institution too strongly to the approval and fostering care of the State.

HORATIO STEBBINS,
A. L. STONE,
C. B. WYATT.

REPORT OF THE COMMITTEE OF EXAMINATION

FOR 1867.

———

To the Board of Directors of the Asylum for Deaf Mutes, and the Blind :

GENTLEMEN : — In pursuance of the duty assigned us, we witnessed and participated in the Annual Examination of the above named Institution, on the 8th day of last month. Having already given a somewhat detailed account of the examinations in both departments through the public press, we content ourselves with the following general statements :

The Blind, in their pursuit of knowledge, are embarrassed by the loss of a sense more important, perhaps, than any other ; yet they have acquired, before entering the Institution, a considerable acquaintance with our own language. In this particular, together with their ability to converse in words, and learn and practice music, they enjoy great advantages over unfortunates of the other class. These are their principal, if not their only advantages. All else, with them, is dark, awkward, and laborious. There are few who adequately appreciate the patience and tact necessary in order to lead their timid feet along the path of progress. The proficiency shown by these pupils, under the immediate care of Mr. Chas. T. Wilkinson, assisted by Miss H. Lovekin, and by Prof. Mueller, in Reading, Mental Arithmetic, Spelling, History, Music, Bead Work, etc., gave proof of abilities and resolute devotion on the part of their teachers. Were it appropriate to consume your time with a repetition of details, the simplest truth would be the highest praise. The accommodations for this department are inconvenient to such a degree as greatly to increase the labor and diminish the success of those into whose charge it is given.

Deaf Mutes enter the Institution almost wholly destitute of language, save that they have picked up unclassified fragments of the sign language in the lower ranges of observation and thought. English is to them what Greek is to more favored children, and they must become acquainted with it by a process more obstructed and laborious than we can adequately conceive of. The same remark applies, substantially, to all the branches which they study. Happily, by a wise modification of policy, peculiar, we believe, or nearly so, to this State, pupils are admitted much younger than has been customary elsewhere, with results so gratifying as to commend in the strongest manner the wisdom of the plan. Some of the pupils, who have enjoyed the instructions of the school steadily and regularly, for several years, exhibit attainments which will aver-age fairly with those of the most privileged scholars of similar ages in the common and select schools in the city. In History and Geography they performed prodigies of memory.

We cannot forbear to express ourselves as peculiarly pleased with the Symbol Grammar introduced by Prof. Wilkinson a little more than a year ago, whose skilled and able Superintendence merits the strongest language of commendation. Under this system three lads, one of them not yet thirteen years of age, analyzed sentences with as much facility and correctness as are usual in the first classes of our grammar schools.

The peculiarly bright, quick-sighted appearance commonly noticeable in mutes, is here heightened by the intellectual discipline to which they are constantly subjected, until it becomes so captivating to the beholder as to supercede, in good part, the saddening effect of their misfortune. Altogether the examinations in this department presented a cheerful and animating scene, full of interesting peculiarities of look and gesture, apprehension and expression.

Your Committee feel that they have rarely been charged with so pleasing a duty as you committed to them, of witnessing the triumph of science and a noble professional devotion over the greatest of physical afflictions. Wherever else we may wisely practice economy by curtailing expenditures, this noble charity of the State must have the most liberal endowments of means and opportunity for the fulfilment of its mission. The present able corps of teachers, animated by the spirit of the accomplished Principal, are deserving of every encouragement which liberality can supply.

Very respectfully, Your Obd't Serv'ts,

E. G. BECKWITH,

M. C. BRIGGS,

Committee.

From the "Evening Bulletin," Sept. 26, 1867.

LAYING OF THE CORNER-STONE FOR THE ASYLUM FOR THE DEAF MUTES
AND THE BLIND.

The ceremonial of laying the corner-stone of the handsome new edifice in course of erection in Alameda county, took place at noon to-day. A large concourse of ladies and gentlemen were gathered together to take part in the interesting exercises attending the ceremony. Upwards of 50 vehicles of all classes, from private carriages to public omnibuses, from San Francisco and Oakland, brought visitors to the ground—besides a great number, especially ladies, who arrived on horseback. The spectators who took most interest in the performance, and were themselves the most interesting to the other spectators, were a party of boys and girls, about 50 in all, from the Asylum. The site of the new Asylum is one of the finest locations on the foothills of the Contra Costa range. The view contains a wide scope of scenery, taking in the San Francisco peninsula from Bay View to Point Lobos, and Marin county from the Golden Gate half way towards the head of San Pablo Bay, with all the islands of the noble Bay of San Francisco filling up the middle of the picture, and the suburban retreat of Oakland and its northern vicinage for a foreground. Some time was spent by the assemblage in examining the foundations of the building and the general arrangement of the interior, which could be almost understood without the explanation of the architects, as the joists of the first floor were laid and all the interior window and door frames were erected in their places. The visitors obtained a very good idea of what the building would be when finished. To further assist them in doing so, a large and handsomely finished perspective drawing of the building, from the pencil of Mr. Sanders, was exhibited on the ground.

WHAT THE ARCHITECTS WERE ASKED TO DO.

Though in thinly populated States like California it is customary to place the deaf and dumb and the blind under one roof, it must be remembered that there is no natural connection, but rather antagonism between them. The motive of placing them in one asylum is simply one of economy. In the new building the architects were asked to design two asylums, so arranged that they could be conducted under one management, with a common dining-room and one culinary department. Not only, however, had the architects to lay out two asylums in one general plan, but in each asylum there had to be perfect separation of the sexes, except at meals, studies and worship, provided for. The Commissioners asked for a plan which should isolate the blind boys from the blind girls, as well as from the mute girls and mute boys, and so on with each class of inmates. Accommodation was to be provided for 120 pupils, 70 deaf and dumb and 50 blind, with capability for enlargement, so as to accommodate 250 pupils, and yet the building externally and internally was to be complete without the extensions. Further, the building was to contain 25,000 feet of flooring, exclusive of halls and passages, and not to exceed $77,000 in cost.

WHAT THE ARCHITECTS HAVE DONE.

This difficult problem of building an asylum which should contain four separate institutions and have an area of flooring of 25,000 superficial feet, was solved by Messrs. Wright & Sanders, and without sacrificing either beauty of design or solidity of work, at an estimate of $80,000. This would have given a building with walls similar in workmanship and material to the Protestant Orphan Asylum in this city. The Commissioners, however, finding that for an increase of $24,000 in the cost they could have masonry of a very superior class, agreed to lay out that additional sum.

DIMENSIONS.

The main building has a frontage of 192 feet by 148 feet deep. The height from the ground line to the top of the gables is 62 feet; to the ridge of the roof and angular towers, is 70 feet. From the ground line to the top of the vane surmounting the spire, is 145 feet. From the foot of the foundation to the ground line, is an average of 12 feet. From the lowest part of the foundation to the vane, 161 feet.

MATERIAL.

The exterior walls, throughout, except the facing of the front, are built of sandstone procured from quarries situate about three-quarters of a mile from the site of the building. The interior partition walls only are brick. The execution is what is technically called random-coursed masonry. The corners of the building and the angles of the buttresses, front, sides and rear of the asylum and interior courts, will have tooled margin-drafts. The window-sills and reveals of the doors and windows, are cut stone-work, as also are the main porch, string courses, copings and chimney-shafts. The facing of the front of the building, throughout, will be of blue stone of fine quality.

FRONT ELEVATION.

The style is domestic Gothic, but of light and cheerful character, with large mullioned and transomed window-openings and buttressed angles. The front elevation consists of a centre three stories and a-half in height, surmounted by a tower. One of the chief features is the porch, which stands boldly out from the main line and supports the projecting work of the middle bay of windows. Extending on each side of the centre are the wings, of two stories and a half in height, finished off with octagonal bays and projecting oriel windows, throwing the plain portion of the wings into recess. The upper tier of windows in the wings are finished with dormer heads, copings and ornamental iron finials. The eaves are enriched with brackets and archlets. The roof-line is broken in the centre and over the bays of the terminating wings by towers in the French style of roofing, finished with elegant iron railings on the flats and crestings on the ridges.

INTERIOR ARRANGEMENTS—GROUND FLOOR.

On entering the building, the visitor will find a museum on his right and a reception-room and library on his left, as he passes through the small hall. In the main hall will stand the grand staircase, with a flight of steps rising from each side and meeting overhead. Underneath and between the two flights, is the door of the dining-saloon. This room occupies the centre of the building on the ground floor, as the chapel does on the upper floor. On the north and south of the dining-saloon are open courts, giving light and air to the building; and in the rear or east is the culinary department. In the four corners of the building, and connected by separate passages with the dining-room on the one floor and with the chapel on the other, are the four suites of apartments which, in reality, are separate institutions. The south-west corner of this floor is the blind girls' sitting-room, with the blind girls' own corridor. In the south-east corner is the deaf mute girls' sitting-room and corridor. In the north-west corner are placed the deaf mute boys' apartments, and in the north-east the blind boys' apartments. The space on the south between the blind girls' and the deaf mute girls' sitting-rooms, is devoted to four class-rooms for the blind. The corresponding space on the north is devoted to class-rooms for the deaf mutes. The intervening area between the apartments of the blind and the deaf mutes in the rear and front, is given up to teachers', matrons and stewards' rooms, all of which open into corridors communicating with the apartments of one or other class of inmates. Each corridor has its separate staircase communicating with the dormitory set apart for the class it belongs to.

UPPER FLOORS.

The dormitories of each class of inmates occupy the two floors, and are immediately over their sitting-rooms. The front and rear of the building is divided into smaller apartments, and contains the teachers' chambers, sick wards, the Principal's suite of rooms, servants' quarters, lavatories and bath-rooms.

PRESENT AND FUTURE ACCOMMODATION.

The building will accommodate 125 pupils, and by raising the class-rooms, which are now one story, to a uniform height with the rest of the building, 250 can be accommodated at a cost of $20,000 additional outlay. When the State shall become suffi-ciently populous to afford a separate asylum for the blind, the building will be found no less convenient than now. The whole of the south end will then be given up to the deaf mute girls, and the north end to the deaf mute boys.

HEATING, LIGHTING AND VENTILATION.

It is proposed to apply the Ensley patent gas company's ap-paratus to the lighting of the building. The heating will be by hot water-pipes, distributing the heat in such portions of the building as may require it from a boiler heated by a furnace near the laundry department. To ensure ventilation, every apartment has one or more gratings communicating with the outer air, and fitted with regulators; and to carry off the foul air there are openings in the ceiling over the gas jets, leading to flues and air ducts leading up to ventilating shafts in the tower.

YARDS AND PLAY-GROUNDS.

Each branch of the institution or class of pupils will have its own play-ground and yard, with ample covered sheds, and there will be direct access to them from the apartments of each class, without interference or contact with the inmates of other portions of the building.

THE ARCHITECTS AND CONTRACTORS.

The architects are Wright & Sanders of 331 Montgomery street. The contractor for the masonry is Mr. Emory. The contractor for the balance of the work is John S. Macredy. The contract was signed at the latter end of July, the builder broke ground the next day, a week later the building commenced. An average height of ten feet above the ground line has been already reached, and it is confidently expected that the building will be finished by July, 1868. In solidity and elegance, the building will have few rivals in the State of California; and should it be finished under the present contracts, will be the cheapest building for its class erected on this coast.

*   *   *   *   *   *   *

*   *   *   *   *   *   *

TERMS OF ADMISSION.

I. The Institution offers its benefits to all Deaf and Dumb, or Blind persons, between the ages of six and twenty-five years, who are of sound intellect and free from vicious habits, and contagious or offensive diseases.

II. No charge is made for pupils from this State, except for clothing and traveling expenses.

III. Pupils from other States or Territories are charged three hundred dollars per annum, payable quarterly in advance. No deduction is made from annual charge, on any account, except in cases of prolonged sickness.

IV. The session begins on the third Wednesday of August, and closes the second Wednesday of June. Parents are urgently requested to enter or return their children promptly at the beginning of the term. Only in extreme cases will the pupils be permitted to leave before school closes.

V. Pupils should be provided with comfortable clothing when they enter the Institution, and their wardrobe renewed twice a year.

VI. All moneys designed for pupils should be placed in the hands of the Principal, to whom, also, all letters of inquiry, etc., should be addressed.

Parents or guardians of applicants for admission are requested to furnish written answers to the following questions :

1. What is the name of the applicant?
2. When and where was he born?
3. Is his deafness or blindness from birth; or is it from accident or disease? If so, at what age and from what cause did he become so?
4. Is his deafness or blindness total or partial? If the latter, what is the degree of hearing or sight?
5. Have any attempts been made to remove his deafness or blindness; and if so, what are the results?
6. Are there any other cases of deafness, blindness, insanity, or idiocy in the same family, or among the collateral branches of kindred? If so, how and when produced?
7. Was there any relation between parents or grandparents before marriage?
8. Has the child had the small pox, scarlet fever, measles, mumps, whooping-cough? Has he been vaccinated?
9. What are the names, occupation, residence, and post office address of his parents?
10. What are the number and names of their children?

.